MW00899255

this book belongs to:

WORLD'S
OKAYEST
VET
TECH

49%
VET TECH
51%
BADASS

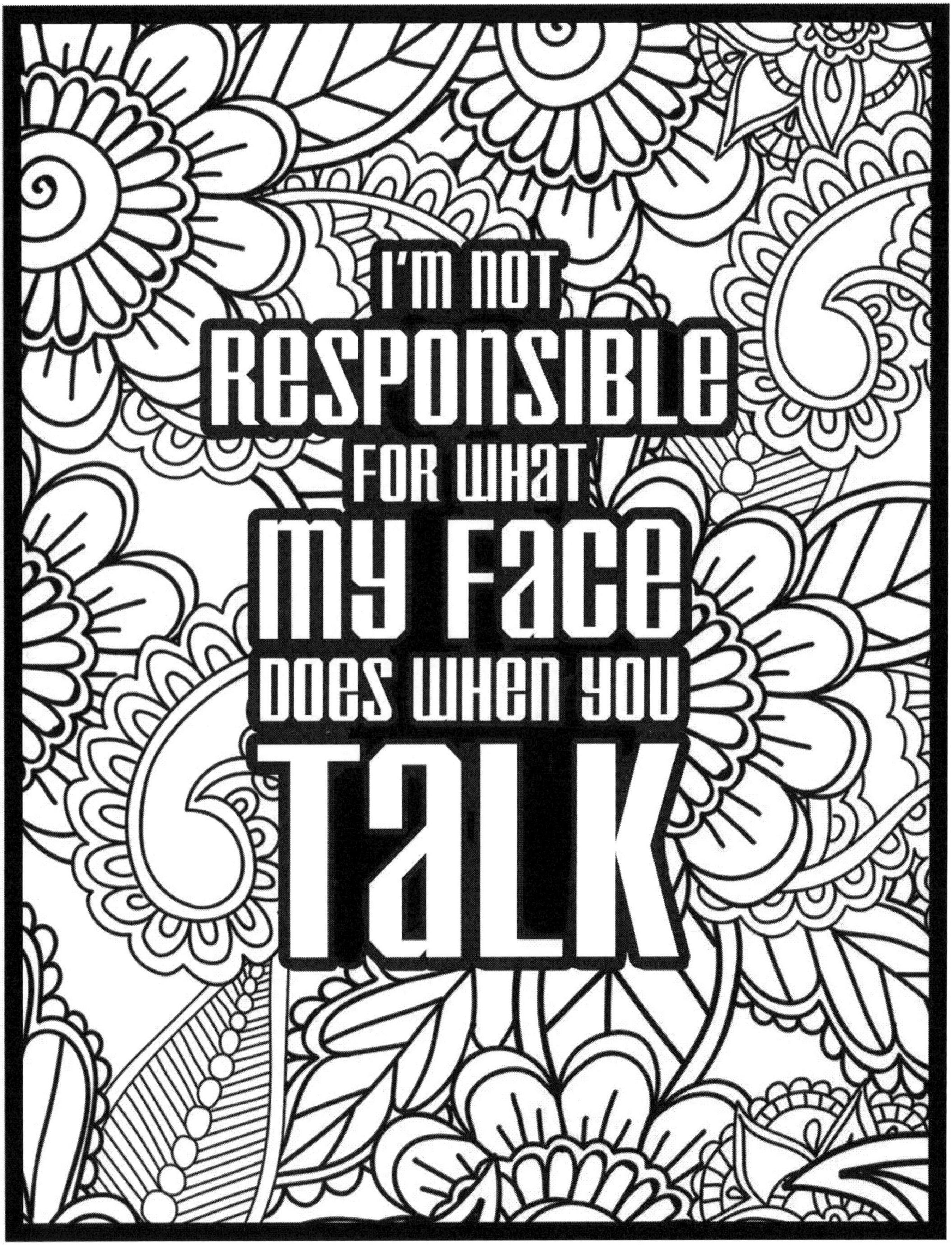
I'M NOT
RESPONSIBLE
FOR WHAT
MY FACE
DOES WHEN YOU
TALK

DON'T MAKE
ME USE MY
Vet Tech
VOICE!

VET TECH
BECAUSE
BADASS
MIRACLE
WORKER
ISN'T AN
OFFICIAL
JOB TITLE

I'VE 99
PROBLEMS
BUT
COLORING
AIN'T ONE

THIS
VET
TECH
IS OFF
DUTY

Sorry
I'M DONE
HELPING
ASSHOLES
Today

I'M A
VET TECH
WHAT'S YOUR
SUPER
POWER?

Three horrible facts:
1- Today is not Friday.
2- Tomorrow is not Friday.
3- Even the day after tomorrow is not Friday.

STFU!
JUST ASSUME
I'M ALWAYS
RIGHT

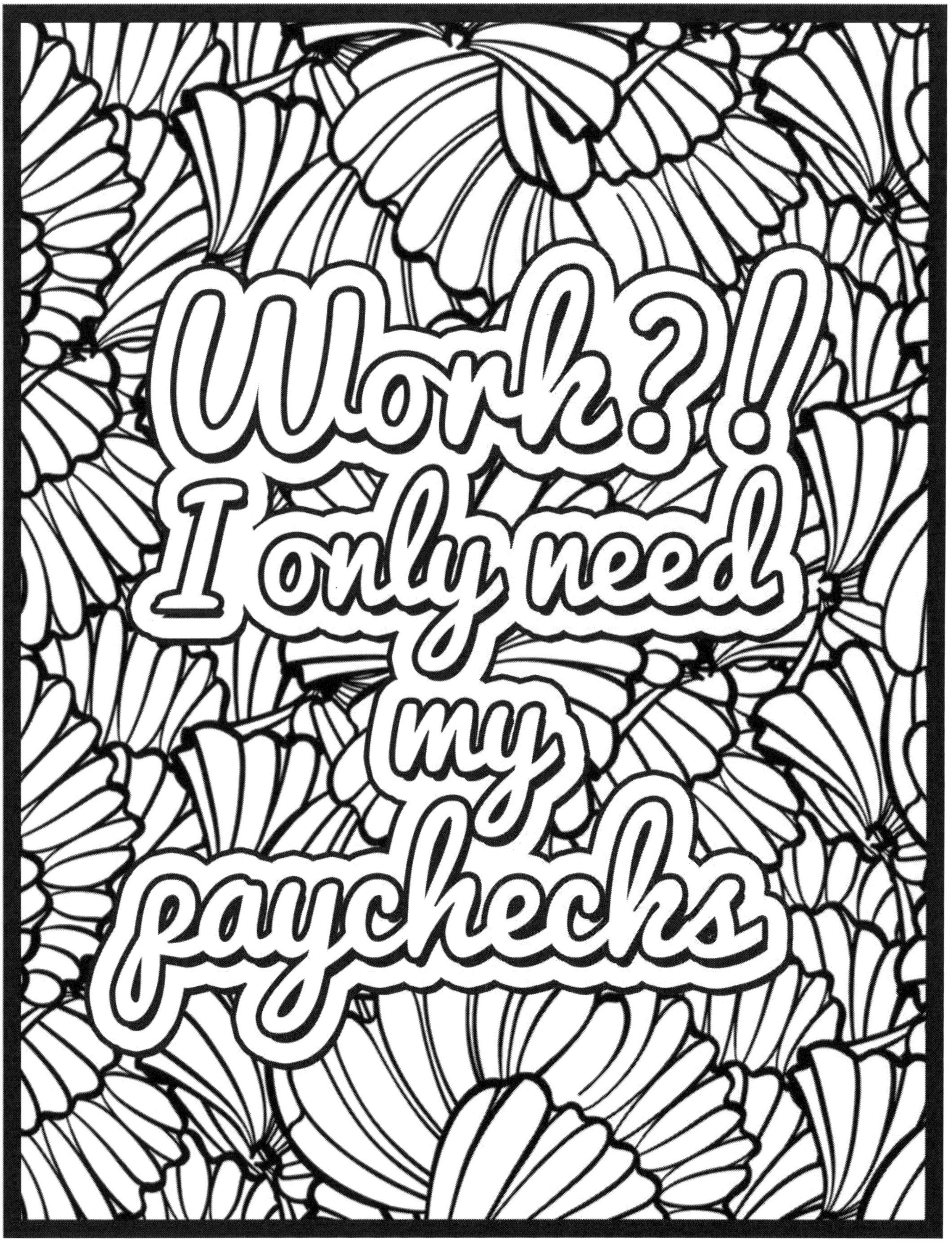
Work?!
I only need
my
paychecks

IT'S A
VET TECH
THING
you'd not
understand

SOME PEOPLE
JUST NEED A
High-Five
(IN THE FACE)

LOOK AT ME
BECOMING A
Vet Tech
AND
SHIT!

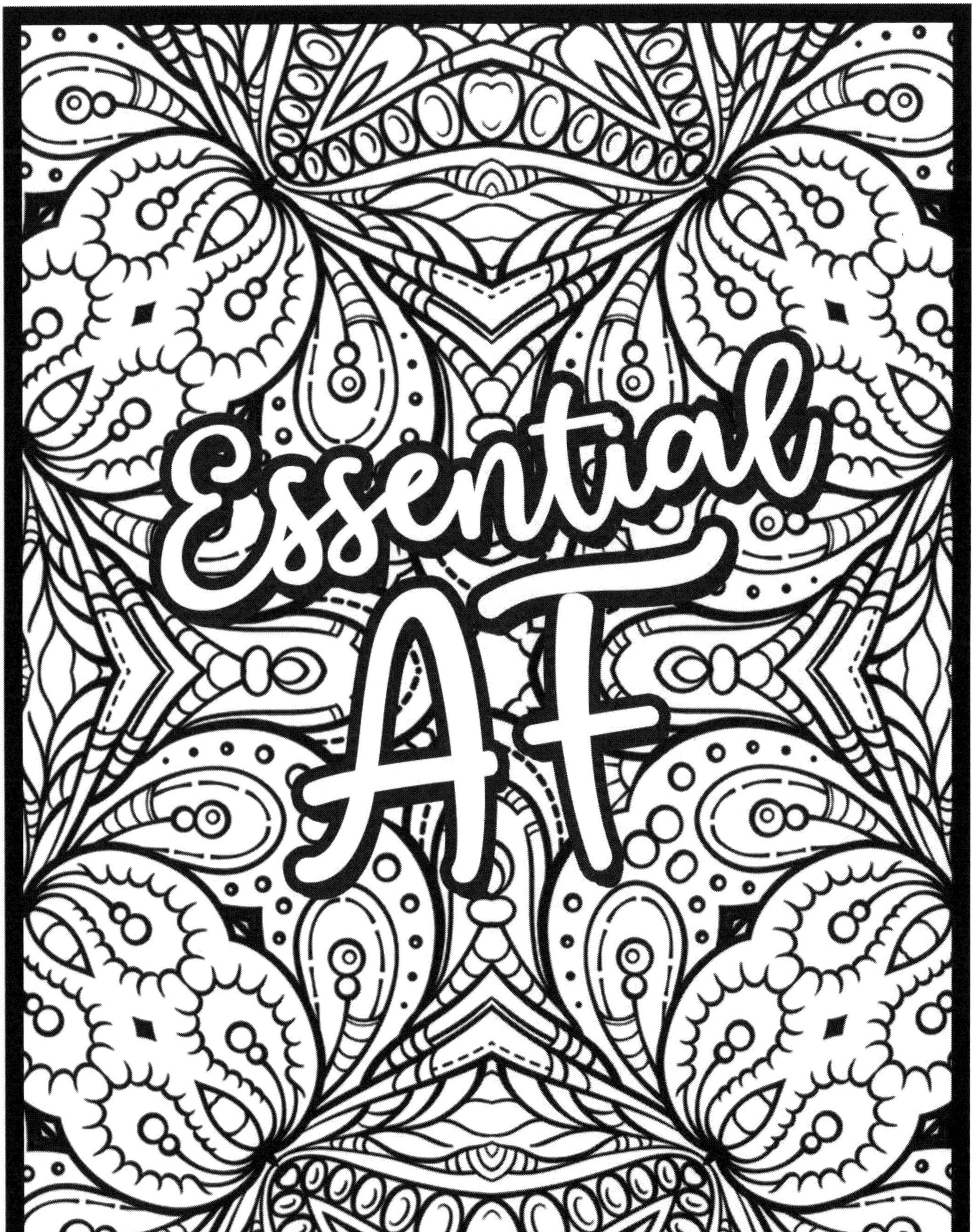
Essential
AF

FRIDAY.
MY SECOND
FAVORITE
F WORD.

This
Vet Tech
Needs a
Mother
Fu*kin'
Drink!

I CAN'T FIX
STUPID
BUT I CAN FIX
WHAT STUPID
DOES

Best
Vet
Tech
Ever

Made in the USA
Las Vegas, NV
31 October 2022

58468172R10024